The Truth Behind This Haggadah

Too many Passover Seders are as dull as plain matzah. At JewBelong, we believe every Jewish event should fill one's soul. Our booklets, including the one in your hand, is one of the ways we make this happen. (People have called us the least judgy/most inclusive Jewish group in the US, and maybe the world.) We need your help to keep going. Even though this Haggadah was free to you (if you ordered it from Amazon, you only paid printing costs) it's expensive for us to maintain and most importantly, to help reach other people who might need the love and inspiration we have to give! Care about a thriving Jewish community? Donate to JewBelong. We'll take it from there. Thank you!

DONATE HERE

♥/ **team jewbelong**

Eight Steps to a Kickass Seder

Too many Seders are dull as matzah! Hosting a fun, thought-provoking Seder is important! Heck, it might be the only Jewish experience of the year for some of your guests! Seems like a lot of pressure, but we've got you with these easy steps for a JewBelong Seder!

Before you get started here are a few extra items you'll want to have on hand: black coffee, dates, an orange, three ingredients for Ruth's Mix: almonds, raisins and chocolate chips.

1) The Seder Police - There Are None.

Yes, there are certain traditions to a Seder. In fact, the word Seder means "order." But if you're the Seder leader, you are the master of the table. If that means starting with the songs, or going right to the skit, do it. But have a game plan. Know which pages you want to spend time on, and definitely assign the skit parts in advance.

2) How Long Should My Seder Be?

As long as possible! (jk), kind of. Some Seders last into the wee hours. Other people rush through it. Frankly, it's hard to fit all of the good parts into a Seder that lasts less than 45 minutes. When you have a fantastic Haggadah (ahem... ours!), you can easily keep a group captivated. The entire JewBelong Haggadah takes about 90 minutes, and between the singing and the skit, it goes really fast!

3) Prepare, Prepare, Prepare.

If Seder leaders spent as much time preparing their Seder service as they do finding a recipe for matzah balls, celebrating Passover could be a lot more meaningful. Seder leaders often think they can just wing it - and they can't.

4) Know Your Audience.

Who's going to be at your Seder? If you're having first-timers, keep that in mind. At JewBelong, we've been going to Seders our entire lives, and it wasn't until we put together our own Haggadah that we really learned the details. If you are hosting a cerebral group and want to go around the room and ask what freedom means to each of them, go right ahead, but that won't work for every crowd. If you're having kids, make sure you either serve appetizers or have snacks on the table. And don't be opposed to setting up *A Rugrats Passover* in another room for those who hit the wall.

5) Haters Gonna Hate.

If you're going to lead a Seder, then someone's got to tell you this, so it might as well be us. There are probably/definitely going to be people at your table who are going to be impatient from the get-go. They might check their watch, they might ask you to skip a reading or two... These are the same people who leave a great concert before the encore. Please, for the love of all that is good and holy, do not let the Haters get under your skin, and don't rush through your Seder because of them. And maybe, don't invite them next year.

6) Watch Out For Too Much Hebrew (aka Don't Play "Who's the Better Jew?").

You know that uncomfortable feeling when you're at a Seder with 18 people, and there are only four who know the words to some Hebrew song, and the rest sit there uncomfortably while they stumble through it? We do too. And it can make people feel like bad Jews. This is NOT the feeling you want to elicit at your Seder. So, if you're going to include Hebrew, make sure your guests understand it, or keep it to a minimum.

7) Centerpieces, Drinking Games & Other Fun Stuff.

The Passover story is loaded with ideas to add even more fun to your Seder! JewBelong.org has instructions to make a Jello Red Sea Centerpiece and Baby Moses in a Basket. But don't stop there! Decorate your table with long reeds so it looks like a sea of reeds, use pillows, because we're supposed to recline because we're no longer slaves, plus gather various props that represent the ten plagues. You can also go big with costumes and props for the skit. Not to mention alcohol. If your guests are of the right age, it's more fun singing Dayeinu a little buzzed. Be creative...Moses Martini anyone? Our JewBelong favorite drinking game is "Burning Bush": Every time you hear the name "Moses" take a shot/sip of Fireball Whiskey.

8) Invite People Now, and Invite Them Again Later.

When is it too early or too late to invite people? Some people already know what their plans are for next year's Passover, because their family always goes to their Aunt Barbara's. Other people are happy to get an invitation to a Passover Seder the morning of! Our advice is go ahead and invite people as soon as you decide you're having a Seder (even those people who always go to their Aunt Barbara's). If you've ever hosted an event before, you know that people aren't always great with the RSVPs, others will cancel last minute, and others will ask to bring their new friend from work/pilates/Hinge. Don't be shy about sending reminders.

Whether it's your first Seder

or your 107th, and whether you've cleaned your home of every last crumb of chametz (food that has leavening), or you plan to eat an English muffin for breakfast tomorrow it doesn't matter. The Seder is a chance for us all to be taken on a short but important journey - from slavery to freedom, and to join millions of Jews and non-Jews all over the world who are doing the same thing. (Think about how cool that is for a second...). The Passover story includes love, deception, belief, hope and freedom. When you get to the skit that tells the story of Passover, imagine yourself wearing dirty rags in the dusty desert of Egypt. Sing loudly during the music moments no matter how you think you sound. Let the readings about freedom open your heart. And, for God's sake, don't worry about the Hebrew (there's barely any in here). Have an extra glass of wine if you want. Just have fun! You're in for a treat. And maybe a bit of a hangover. **Happy Passover!**

team jewbelong

As we begin tonight's Seder

let's take a moment to be thankful for being together. We make a small community of storytellers. But, why this story again? Most of us already know the story of Passover. The answer is that we are not merely telling a story. We are being called to the act of empathy. Some at our table observe this holiday every year and some are experiencing it for the first time. Some of us are Jewish, others are not. Passover is enjoyed by people of various faiths because freedom is at the core of each of our stories. All who are in need, let them come celebrate Passover with us. Now we are here. Next year in the land of Israel.

Ruth's Mix

Ruth, as in "The Book of", as in the great-grandmother of King David, was part of an interfaith marriage. Ruth's Mix welcomes everyone to the Seder table and honors the growing diversity of the Jewish people – those who were born Jewish, those who converted, those who are not Jewish, and those who just came for the singing and wine. Everyone takes a bit of Ruth's Mix, a combination of almonds, raisins and chocolate chips. Each of these ingredients is good on its own, but when mixed together they're even better.

Blessing for anyone who isn't Jewish ('cause we know this is a lot)

May everyone who shares in a Jewish life feel welcome and integrated. We lovingly acknowledge the diversity of our community and are deeply grateful for the love and support you provide by opening your heart to Judaism, no matter how big or small a part it is in your day. Your presence at this Jewish experience is valued. It is not taken for granted because not everyone in this broken world will sit at a Shabbat dinner or attend a Passover Seder. We are a very small people and history has made us smaller. As we once again see a rise in hatred and hear fear in the voices of our community, we are grateful for your presence. We pray with all our hearts that all you give to the Jewish people will come back to you and fill your life with joy. Amen.

For Those Raising Kids: We offer special thanks to those who are raising their sons and daughters with Jewish identity. Our children mean hope, life and future. With all our hearts, we want to thank you for your love and willingness in giving the ultimate gift to the Jewish people. Amen.
-Adapted from Rabbi Janet Marder

Wait! Before we go on... Can we talk about the elephant at the Seder table?

He's demanding our attention and we need to give it to him, because it is a matter of life and death. The elephant is antisemitism. There's the familiar white supremacy movement that hates everyone who doesn't look like them. The more subtle I-don't-really-mean-it-when-I-talk-crap-about-Jews kind. And of course the insidious form of hostility directed at Israel, which crosses the line to antisemitism far too often. Hate is hate. Jews, Christians, Muslims, Hindus, atheists... everyone is worse off for it. Are we going to end it? No. We must talk about it, write about it, learn about it, and call it out. Those who wish to erase Israel and the Jewish people are relentless. This is a time that Jews and allies must work just as hard.

Now that we've acknowledged the elephant, let's not let him plunder the table. If we do, we'll never get to the Four Questions, and besides, the matzah ball soup will get cold. Seders end with the phrase Next Year in Jerusalem. We may be going out on a limb here, but we're guessing that most of us won't be in Jerusalem next year.
We'll probably be sitting right here. But we can't take that for granted.
We've already learned the bitter lesson that antisemitism is never little, it is never unimportant, and it should never, ever be ignored.

And now, a song

TAKE US OUT OF EGYPT
(To the tune of "Take Me Out to the Ball Game")

Take us out of Egypt,
Free us from slavery.
Bake us some matzah, in a haste
Don't worry 'bout flavor,
Give no thought to taste

Oh it's RUSH, RUSH, RUSH,
To the Red Sea
If we don't cross it's a shame —

For it's TEN PLAGUES,
Down and you're out
At the Pesach game!!!

Passover Remembered
(Everyone read one bullet)

- Pack nothing. Bring only your determination to serve and your willingness to be free.
- Don't wait for the bread to rise. Take nourishment for the journey, but eat standing, be ready to move at a moment's notice.
- Do not hesitate to leave your old ways behind – fear, silence, submission.
- Do not take time to explain to the neighbors. Tell only a few trusted friends and family members.
- Then begin quickly, before you have time to sink back into the old slavery.
- Set out in the dark. I will send fire to warm and encourage you. I will be with you in the fire, and I will be with you in the cloud.
- You will learn to eat new food and find refuge in new places. I will give you dreams in the desert to guide you safely home to that place you have not yet seen.
- The stories you tell one another around your fires in the dark will make you strong and wise.
- Outsiders will attack you, some will follow you, and at times you will be weary and turn on each other from fear and fatigue and blind forgetfulness.
- You have been preparing for this for hundreds of years. I am sending you into the wilderness to make your way and to learn my ways more deeply.
- Those who fight you will teach you. Those who fear you will strengthen you. Those who follow you may forget you. Only be faithful. This alone matters.
- Some of you will die in the desert, for the way is longer than anyone imagined. Some of you will give birth.
- Some will join other tribes along the way, and some will simply stop and create new families in a welcoming oasis.
- Some of you will be so changed by weathers and wanderings that even your closest friends will have to learn your features as though for the first time.
- Some of you will not change at all.
- Sing songs as you go, and hold close together. You may, at times, grow confused and lose your way.
- Continue to call each other by the names I've given you to help remember who you are. You will get where you are going by remembering who you are.
- Tell your children lest they forget and fall into danger – remind them even if they were not born in freedom but under a bondage they no longer remember, which is still with them, if unseen.
- So long ago you fell into slavery, slipped into it unaware, out of hunger and need.
- Do not let your children sleep through the journey's hardship. Keep them awake and walking on their own feet so that you both remain strong and on course.
- So you will be only the first of many waves of deliverance on these desert seas. Do not go back.
- I am with you now and I am waiting for you.

THERE'S NO SEDER LIKE OUR SEDER

To the tune of "There's No Business Like Show Business"

There's no Seder like our Seder,
Like no Seder I know.

Everything about it is halachic
Nothing that the Torah won't allow.

Listen how we read the whole Haggadah
It's all in Hebrew 'cause we know how.

There's no Seder like our Seder,
We tell a tale that is swell;
Moses took the people out into the heat
They baked the matzah
While on their feet
Now isn't that a story
That just can't be beat?
Let's go on with the show!

Seder = Order

Our Passover meal is called a Seder, which means "order" in Hebrew, because we go through 14 specific steps as we retell the story of our ancestors' liberation from slavery in Egypt.

1. Kiddush Blessing Over Wine — **KADEISH** קַדֵּשׁ
2. Ritual Hand-Washing (first): Preparing for the Seder — **URCHATZ** וּרְחַץ
3. Dipping Greens in Salt Water — **KARPAS** כַּרְפַּס
4. Breaking the Middle Matzah — **YACHATZ** יַחַץ
5. Telling the Story of Passover — **MAGGID** מַגִּיד
6. Ritual Hand-Washing (second): Preparing for the Meal — **RACHTZAH** רָחְצָה
7. Blessing Over Meal and Matzah — **MOTZI MATZAH** מוֹצִיא מַצָּה
8. Dipping the Bitter Herb in Sweet Charoset — **MAROR** מָרוֹר
9. Eating Matzah/Bitter Herb Sandwich — **KOREICH** כּוֹרֵךְ
10. Eating the Meal — **SHULCHAN OREICH** שֻׁלְחָן עוֹרֵךְ
11. Finding and Eating the Afikomen — **TZAFUN** צָפוּן
12. Saying Grace After Meal, Inviting in Elijah — **BAREICH** בָּרֵךְ
13. Singing Songs That Praise God — **HALLEL** הַלֵּל
14. Ending the Seder and Thinking About the Future — **NIRTZAH** נִרְצָה

🎵 OUR PASSOVER THINGS
To the tune of "My Favorite Things"

And one more song!

Cleaning and cooking and so many dishes
Out with the chametz, no pasta, no knishes
Fish that's gefillted, horseradish that stings
These are a few of our Passover things.

Matzah and karpas and chopped up charoset
Shankbones and Kiddush and Yiddish neurosis
Tante who kvetches and uncle who sings
These are a few of our Passover things.

When the plagues strike
When the lice bite
When we're feeling sad
We simply remember our Passover things
And then we don't feel so bad.

Motzi and maror and trouble with Pharaohs
Famines and locusts and slaves with wheelbarrows
Matzah balls floating and eggshells that cling
These are a few of our Passover things.

When the plagues strike
When the lice bite
When we're feeling sad
We simply remember our Passover things
And then we don't feel so bad.

Candle Lighting Blessing The Light

The day ends. The earth turns from sunshine to dusk and then to darkness. We assume for ourselves the task of kindling candles in the night, to enlighten the dark corners of our world. We still live in perilous times. Behind us, though receding into the memories of even the oldest among us, we can still sense the fires of Auschwitz. We gather tonight to create from fire, not the heat of destruction, but the light of instruction; indeed to see more clearly the wisdom, strength and caring that glows from within each of us.

TOGETHER: May these candles, lit on the Festival of Freedom, bring light into our hearts and minds. May they renew our courage to act for justice and freedom here and now. May they illuminate the path of truth, justice and peace.

בָּרוּךְ אַתָּה ה' אֱלֹהֵינוּ מֶלֶךְ הָעוֹלָם אֲשֶׁר קִדְּשָׁנוּ בְּמִצְוֹתָיו וְצִוָּנוּ לְהַדְלִיק נֵר שֶׁל [שַׁבָּת וְשֶׁל] יוֹם טוֹב.

Baruch atah Adonai, Eloheinu Melech ha-olam,
asher kiddishanu b'mitzvotav, v'tzivanu lehadlik neir shel [Shabbat v'shel] Yom Tov. Amen.

We praise God, Spirit of Everything, who has directed us to kindle [the Shabbat] and holiday lights.

1. Kiddush Blessing Over Wine:
The First Glass of Wine

Fill your cup with the first glass of wine, lift the cup, say the Kiddush, and drink. All Jewish celebrations, from holidays to weddings, include wine as a symbol of our joy – not to mention a practical way to increase that joy. The Seder starts with the first cup of wine and then gives us three more opportunities to refill our cup and drink.

בָּרוּךְ אַתָּה ה', אֱלֹהֵינוּ מֶלֶךְ הָעוֹלָם בּוֹרֵא פְּרִי הַגָּפֶן.

Baruch atah Adonai, Eloheinu Melech ha-olam borei p'ri hagafen.

We praise God, Spirit of Everything, creator of the fruit of the vine.

And now we drink.

Shehecheyanu

At JewBelong we think of the Shehecheyanu as a catch-all/generic prayer of gratitude, which makes it perfect for Passover.

בָּרוּךְ אַתָּה ה', אֱלֹהֵינוּ מֶלֶךְ הָעוֹלָם, שֶׁהֶחֱיָנוּ וְקִיְּמָנוּ וְהִגִּיעָנוּ לַזְּמַן הַזֶּה.

Baruch atah Adonai, Eloheinu Melech ha-olam, she-hechiayanu v'key'manu v'higiyanu lazman hazeh. Amen.

We praise God, Spirit of Everything, who has kept us alive, raised us up and brought us to this moment.

The Seder Plate
The Seder Plate holds the ritual items discussed during the Seder.

Roasted Shankbone One of the most striking symbols of Passover is the roasted lamb shankbone (called zeroah), which commemorates the paschal (lamb) sacrifice made the night the ancient Hebrews fled Egypt. Some say it symbolizes the outstretched arm of God (the Hebrew word zeroah can mean "arm"). Many vegetarians use a roasted beet instead. This isn't a new idea; the great Biblical commentator Rashi suggested it back in the eleventh century.

Maror (Bitter Herb) Bitter herbs (usually horseradish) bring tears to the eyes and recall the bitterness of slavery. The Seder refers to the slavery in Egypt, but people are called to look at their own bitter enslavements.

Charoset There's nothing further from maror than charoset, the sweet salad of apples, nuts, wine, and cinnamon that represents the mortar used by the Hebrew slaves to make bricks.

Karpas Karpas is a green vegetable, usually parsley (though any spring green will do). Karpas symbolizes the freshness of spring. Some families still use boiled potatoes for karpas, continuing a tradition from Eastern Europe where it was difficult to find fresh green vegetables.

Salt Water Salt water symbolizes the tears and sweat of our ancestors who were slaves.

Orange The orange is a symbol of the fruitfulness and inclusion of LGBTQ+ members of the Jewish community. We spit out the seeds of homophobia and welcome all who feel marginalized.

Roasted Egg The roasted egg (baytsah) is a symbol in many different cultures, usually signifying springtime and renewal. Here it stands in place of one of the sacrificial offerings performed in the days of the Second Temple. Another popular interpretation is that the egg is like the Jewish people: the hotter you make it for them, the tougher they get.

Boiled Egg (To eat) At many seders an egg that has been dipped in salt water is eaten. Recite this short blessing before eating the egg.

TOGETHER: May we reflect on our lives this year and soften our hearts to those around us. Another year has passed since we gathered at the Seder table, and we are once again reminded that life is fleeting. We are reminded to use each precious moment wisely so that no day will pass without bringing us closer to some worthy achievement as we all take a moment to be aware of how truly blessed we are.

Blessing for Israel

Date palm trees are known for their resilience and ability to thrive in arid climates, and they stand for perseverance, abundance and growth. The same can be said for our brothers and sisters in Israel. Take a date before reading this next blessing:

May our family in Israel be free, and those who are still being held hostage, in body or spirit, feel the strength of our love. May the families and loved ones of the hostages feel our support. We pray that the soldiers who are fighting on behalf of all of us feel our love. These brave young men and women are defending Israel, the only safe haven for the Jewish people, and paying the price in time lost with family, financial hardship, permanent damage to their bodies and minds, and their lives. And we are here, in the safety of our homes, celebrating the freedom of the Jewish people. The irony is palpable.

May the sweetness of the dates help us connect even more greatly to their sacrifices while reminding us of the resilience of Israel and the Jewish people throughout history. As we celebrate the story of liberation, let us pray for a future of peace. Amen.

And now, a really fun song!

🎵 PASSOVER ROUND
To the Tune of Frére Jacques

A round is a short musical piece in which multiple voices sing the same melody but start the song at different times. When each singer/group gets to the end of the song, they return to the beginning and start again!

Roasted Shankbone, Roasted Shankbone
Hard-boiled Egg, Hard-boiled Egg
Karpas and Charoset, Karpas and Charoset
Bitter Herbs, Bitter Herbs

Repeat 2 or 3 times!

A Time of Remembering

On this Seder night, we recall with anguish and love our martyred brothers and sisters, the six million Jews of Europe who were destroyed at the hands of a tyrant more fiendish than Pharaoh. Their memory will never be forgotten.

Trapped in ghettos, caged in death camps, abandoned by an unseeing or uncaring world, Jews gave their lives in acts that sanctified God's name and the name of the people of Israel. Some rebelled against their tormentors, fighting with makeshift weapons, gathering the last remnants of their failing strength in peerless gestures of courage and defiance. Others went to their death with their faith in God miraculously unimpaired.

Unchecked and unchallenged, evil ran rampant and devoured the holy innocents. But the light of the six million will never be extinguished. Their glow illuminates our path. We will teach our children and our children's children to remember them with reverence and with pride.

Bashert (Destiny)

These Words Are Dedicated to Those Who Died

Because they had no love and felt alone in the world
Because they were afraid to be alone and tried
to stick it out
Because they could not ask
Because they were shunned
Because they were sick and their bodies could
not resist disease
Because they played it safe
Because they had no connection
Because they had no faith
Because they felt they did not belong and
wanted to die

These Words Are Dedicated to Those Who Died

Because they were loners and liked it
Because they acquired friends and
drew others to them
Because they drew attention to themselves
and always got picked
Because they took risks
Because they were too stubborn and
refused to give up
Because they asked for too much

These Words Are Dedicated to Those Who Died

Because a card was lost
and a number was skipped
Because a bed was denied
Because a place was filled
and no other was left

These Words Are Dedicated to Those Who Died

Because someone did not follow through
Because someone was overworked and forgot
Because someone left everything to God
Because someone was late
Because someone did not arrive at all
Because someone told them to wait and they just
couldn't any longer

These Words Are Dedicated to Those Who Died

Because death is a punishment
Because death is a reward
Because death is the final rest
Because death is eternal rage

These Words Are Dedicated to Those Who Survived

Because their second grade teacher
gave them books
Because they did not draw attention to themselves
and got lost in the shuffle
Because they knew someone who knew someone
else who could help them and
bumped into them on a corner on
a Thursday afternoon
Because they played it safe
Because they took risks
Because they were lucky

These Words Are Dedicated to Those Who Survived

Because they knew how to cut corners
Because they drew attention to themselves and
always got picked
Because they had no principles and were hard

These Words Are Dedicated to Those Who Survived

Because they refused to give up
and defied statistics
Because they had faith and trusted in God
Because they expected the worst and
were always prepared
Because they were angry
Because they could ask
Because they mooched off of others and saved
their strength
Because they endured humiliation
Because they turned the other cheek
Because they looked the other way

These Words Are Dedicated to Those Who Survived

Because life is a wilderness and they were savage
Because life is an awakening and they were alert
Because life is a flowering and they blossomed
Because life is a struggle and they struggled
Because life is a gift and they were free to accept it

These Words Are Dedicated to Those Who Survived.
Bashert.

- Irena Klepfisz

Readings on Freedom

• They marched us down the length of Pozohony Street, toward the Margaret Bridge and that was when we understood they were bringing us to the edge of the Danube, where they would shoot us and leave us to die under the ice. When we arrived at the foot of the bridge, a Soviet reconnaissance aircraft appeared out of nowhere over our heads. The death march stopped, and there was a moment of chaos while the Nazi guards sought refuge in the entrance to buildings and shot their submachine guns skyward. Mother and I were standing next to a small public toilet of metal and painted green and mother pushed me inside.

• "Pretend you're peeing," she said. I stood there frozen with cold and fear, but I could not pee; when you are thirteen years old and frightened, you cannot pee. The Soviet plane had meanwhile disappeared and the march resumed. Not a soul noticed that mother and I had remained in the toilet. Half an hour later, not a single person from the march was left alive. This was a key moment in my life, the moment that defines me more accurately than any other – more than anything I ever did, more than any place I ever visited, more than any person I have ever met. Not because I was spared – every survivor has his own story or a private miracle – but because I had nowhere to go... in this big wide world there was not a single place for a Jewish boy of thirteen whom everyone wants to kill.

• So we went back to the ghetto. Years later on a trip I took to Budapest with my son Yair, we took a walk and found ourselves, without planning to, at the Margaret Bridge. We strolled along, chatting merrily when suddenly I stopped and, shaking, pointed at something ahead of us. At first Yair could not understand what it was that I was pointing at, but there it was: the public toilet made of metal and painted green. We stood there, two grown men, hugging and crying and stroking the green walls of the public toilet that saved my life, while the Hungarians who passed us on the street did so with caution, convinced they were looking at two lunatics.

• "My boy," I said once I was calm enough to speak, "it was in this place, without my even knowing it that I became a Zionist. It is the whole Zionist idea, in fact. The State of Israel is a problematic place, and we'll always have our arguments with it, but this is the very reason it was established. So that every Jewish child will always have a place to go." I hope that Yair understood. I am certain that he did not forget.
-*Memories After My Death: The Story of My Father, Joseph "Tommy" Lapid, by Yair Lapid*

This Year We Are Slaves

• What do these words mean? We are slaves because yesterday our people were in slavery and memory makes yesterday real for us. We are slaves because today there are still people in chains around the world and no one can be truly free while others are in chains.

• We are slaves because freedom means more than broken chains. Where there is poverty and hunger and homelessness, there is no freedom; where there is prejudice and bigotry and discrimination, there is no freedom; where there is violence and torture and war, there is no freedom.

• And where each of us is less than he or she might be, we are not free, not yet. And who, this year, can be deaf to the continuing oppression of the downtrodden, who can be blind to the burdens and the rigors that are now to be added to the most vulnerable in our midst? If these things be so, who among us can say that he or she is free?

What Happens to Them Happens to Me

LEADER: Prejudice is like a monster that has many heads, an evil which requires many efforts to overcome. One head sends forth poison against the people of a different race, another against the people of a different religion or culture. Thus the evil of prejudice is indivisible.

GROUP: Human progress never rolls in on the wheels of inevitability. It comes through the tireless efforts and the persistent work of dedicated individuals who are willing to be co-workers with God. Without this hard work, time itself becomes an ally of the insurgent and primitive forces of irrational emotionalism and social stagnation.

LEADER: What is called for is not a silent sigh but a voice of moral compassion and indignation, the sublime and inspired screaming of a prophet uttered by a whole community.

GROUP: The voice of justice is stronger than bigotry and the hour calls for that voice, as well as, the concerted and incessant action.

LEADER: I have personal faith. I believe firmly that in spite of the difficulties of these days, in spite of the struggles ahead, we can solve this problem. I believe there will be a better world.
-*Martin Luther King Jr. and Abraham J. Heschel*

Especially This Year, A Prayer for Our Country

• Our God and God of our ancestors, bless this country and all who dwell within it. Help us to experience the blessings of our lives and circumstances, to be vigilant, compassionate, and brave. Strengthen us when we are afraid, help us to channel our anger, so that it motivates us to action.

• Help us to be humble in our fear, knowing that as vulnerable as we feel, there are those at greater risk, and that it is our holy work to stand with them. Help us to taste the sweetness of liberty, to not take for granted the freedoms won in generations past. Source of all life, guide our leaders with righteousness, that they may use their influence and authority to speak truth and act for justice. May all who dwell in this country enjoy its freedoms, and be protected by its laws. May this nation use its power and wealth to be a voice for justice, peace, and equality for all who dwell on earth.

• May we be strong and have courage to be bold in our action and deep in our compassion, to uproot bigotry, intolerance, and violence in all its forms, to celebrate the many faces of God reflected in the wondrous diversity of humanity, to welcome the stranger and the immigrant and to honor the gift of those who seek refuge and possibility here, as they have since before this nation was born. Let justice well up like waters, and righteousness like a mighty stream. Amen. *-Adapted from Rabbi Ayelet Cohen*

2. Urchatz Ritual Hand-Washing (first):
Preparation for Seder

Water is refreshing, cleansing and clear, so it's easy to understand why so many cultures and religions use water for symbolic purification. Washing hands can take place twice during our Seder: now, with no blessing to get us ready for the rituals to come; and then later, with a blessing, to prepare us for the meal.

3. Karpas Dipping a Green Vegetable in Salt Water

Passover, like many of our holidays, combines the celebration of an event from our Jewish memory with recognition of the cycles of nature. As we remember the liberation from Egypt, we also recognize the stirrings of spring and rebirth happening in the world around us. We now take a vegetable, representing spring, and dip it into salt water, a symbol of the tears our ancestors shed as slaves. Before we eat it, we recite a short blessing:

בָּרוּךְ אַתָּה ה׳, אֱלֹהֵינוּ מֶלֶךְ הָעוֹלָם, בּוֹרֵא פְּרִי הָאֲדָמָה.

Baruch atah Adonai, Eloheinu Melech ha-olam, borei p'ree ha-adama.

We praise God, Spirit of Everything, who creates the fruits of the earth.

4. Yachatz Breaking the Middle Matzah

• Uncover and hold up the three pieces of matzah and say together: This is the bread of poverty, which our ancestors ate in the land of Egypt. All who are hungry, come and eat; all who are needy, come and celebrate Passover with us. This year we are here; next year we will be in Israel. This year we are slaves; next year we will be free.

• We eat matzah in memory of the quick flight of our ancestors from Egypt. As slaves, they faced many false starts before finally being let go. So when the word of their freedom came, they took whatever dough they had and ran before it had the chance to rise, leaving it looking something like matzah.

• There are three pieces of matzah stacked on the table. We now break the middle matzah into two pieces. One piece is called the Afikomen, literally "dessert" in Greek. The Afikomen is hidden and must be found before the Seder can be finished.

The Four Questions

The telling of the story of Passover is framed as a discussion with questions and answers. The tradition that the youngest person asks the questions reflects the idea of involving everyone at the Seder.

מַה נִּשְׁתַּנָּה הַלַּיְלָה הַזֶּה מִכָּל הַלֵּילוֹת

Ma nishtana halaila hazeh mikol haleilot?

Why is this night different from all other nights?

1

שֶׁבְּכָל הַלֵּילוֹת אָנוּ אוֹכְלִין חָמֵץ וּמַצָּה, הַלַּיְלָה הַזֶּה – כֻּלּוֹ מַצָּה.

Shebichol haleilot anu ochlin chameitz u-matzah. Halaila hazeh kulo matzah.

Why is it that on all other nights during the year we eat either bread or matzah, but on this night we eat only matzah?

2

שֶׁבְּכָל הַלֵּילוֹת אָנוּ אוֹכְלִין שְׁאָר יְרָקוֹת – הַלַּיְלָה הַזֶּה (כֻּלּוֹ) מָרוֹר.

Shebichol haleilot anu ochlin shi'ar yirakot haleila hazeh maror.

Why is it that on all other nights we eat all kinds of herbs, but on this night we eat only bitter herbs?

3

שֶׁבְּכָל הַלֵּילוֹת אֵין אָנוּ מַטְבִּילִין אֲפִילוּ פַּעַם אֶחָת – הַלַּיְלָה הַזֶּה שְׁתֵּי פְעָמִים.

Shebichol haleilot ain anu matbilin afilu pa-am echat.
Halaila hazeh shtei fi-amim.

Why is it that on all other nights we do not dip our herbs even once, but on this night we dip them twice?

4

שֶׁבְּכָל הַלֵּילוֹת אָנוּ אוֹכְלִין בֵּין יוֹשְׁבִין וּבֵין מְסֻבִּין – הַלַּיְלָה הַזֶּה כֻּלָּנוּ מְסֻבִּין.

Shebichol haleilot anu ochlin bein yoshvin uvein m'subin.
Halaila hazeh kulanu m'subin.

Why is it that on all other nights we eat either sitting or reclining, but on this night we eat in a reclining position?

The Four Children (Classic Version)

As we tell the story, we think about it from all angles. Our tradition speaks of four different types of children who react individually to the Passover Seder. It is our job to make our story accessible to all the members of our community:

What does the wise child say?
The wise child asks, What are the testimonies and laws which God commanded you?
You must teach this child the rules of observing the holiday of Passover.

What does the wicked child say?
The wicked child asks, What does this service mean to you? To you and not to himself! Because he takes himself out of the community and misses the point, say to him: "It is because of what God did for me in taking me out of Egypt." Me, not him. Had that child been there, he would have been left behind.

What does the simple child say?
The simple child asks, What is this? To this child, answer plainly: " With a strong hand God took us out of Egypt, where we were slaves."

What about the child who doesn't know how to ask a question?
Help this child ask. Start telling the story: "It is because of what God did for me in taking me out of Egypt."

The Four (Modern) Children

Following is a new interpretation of The Four Children that illustrates the journey of many Jews living in America. We're not judging here, just witnessing. Besides, what better time to talk about choices and change than Passover?

The First Son (Previously Known as the Wise Child)
Let's call him Irving. He came to America in the early 1900s, not only because his family had a terribly poor existence in Poland, but mostly because they were running for their lives to escape the pogroms (vicious riots when gangs of Russian Cossacks went into Jewish shtetls, or villages, and raped and killed thousands of Jews). Irving, and thousands like him, came to America. They came with nothing, but at least America gave them safety and freedom. Irving flourished. As a boy, he spoke Yiddish and went to yeshiva (an orthodox school). When he arrived in America, he learned English. His family remained observant, continuing to follow kosher rules, celebrating Shabbat each week and living a traditional Jewish life. Irving's commitment to Judaism was unshakable.

The Second Daughter (Previously Known as the Wicked Child)
Irving's daughter, Alice, is the second generation. Alice grew up in America with a strong Jewish identity. She's comfortable in her mom and dad's home, which is filled with Jewish traditions and values, but her own home and family are let's just say, more American. Alice experienced some antisemitism, but never felt she had to run for her life. Her goal was to be a successful business executive, and if that meant working on Shabbat, something that Irving would never do, Alice did it. She became so successful that she was one of the first Jews to be accepted into her local country club that would never allow Jews before. Alice took her family to Paris and Rome but forgot to take them to Israel. She did a great job of assimilating, but sort of a lackluster job of teaching her son, Josh, who you will meet below, about Judaism.

The Third Son (Previously Known as the Simple Child)
Meet Alice's son, Josh. He's the third generation of Jews in America. Josh is like, well, lots of us. He considers himself culturally Jewish. Josh may have had a Seder at his grandfather Irving's house, but Josh, who by the way, is an excellent soccer player, never really concentrated on his Judaism. He felt very little antisemitism growing up; he quit Hebrew school because it conflicted with soccer practice, and he went to Hillel a couple of times at Duke (see, told you Josh wasn't simple) but it felt too Jewish for him. Josh did go on Birthright but that was a few years ago. Alice is bummed that Josh doesn't have a stronger connection to Judaism, but what are you gonna do? By the way, Josh is married to Shannon, who is Protestant but would like to learn about Judaism. Unfortunately, Josh doesn't feel like he knows enough to teach her.

The Fourth Daughter (Previously Known as the Child Who Didn't Know How to Ask a Question)
Finally, meet Josh and Shannon's daughter, Luca. Of course, she knows her dad is Jewish, and actually loves seeing old photographs of Irving, but other than that, she has little connection to Judaism. We really miss and need all Lucas! Let's work together to invite everyone who is disengaged from their Judaism, back to our sometimes dysfunctional, often confusing, but always loving community.

What If God Hadn't Taken Our Ancestors Out of Egypt?

Then we would still be enslaved to Pharaoh in Egypt, along with our children, and our children's children. Even if all of us were wise, all of us discerning, all of us scholars, and all of us knowledgeable in Torah, it would still be a mitzvah for us to retell the story of the Exodus from Egypt.

Sing it like you mean it!!

PHARAOH PHARAOH
To the tune of "Louie Louie"

Pharaoh, Pharaoh! Oh baby! Let my people go!
Yeah! Yeah! Yeah! Yeah!
Singin' Pharaoh, Pharaoh! Oh baby!
Let my people go!
Yeah! Yeah! Yeah! Yeah!

A burnin' bush told me just the other day
That I should come over here and stay
Gotta get my people outta Pharaoh's hands
Gotta lead my people to the Promised Land.

The Nile turned to blood!
There were darkened black skies! Gnats and frogs!
There were locusts and flies! The first born died, causing Egypt to grieve,
Finally Pharaoh said, "Y'all can leave!"

Me and my people goin' to the Red Sea
Pharaoh's army's comin' after me.
I raised my rod, stuck it in the sand
All of God's people walked across the dry land.

Pharaoh, Pharaoh! Oh baby! Let my people go!
Yeah! Yeah! Yeah! Yeah!
Singin' Pharaoh, Pharaoh! Oh baby! Let my people go!
Yeah! Yeah! Yeah! Yeah!

Pharaoh's army was a-comin' too
So what do you think that I did do?
Well, I raised my rod and I cleared my throat
All of Pharaoh's army did the dead man's float.

Pharaoh, Pharaoh! Oh baby! Let my people go!
Yeah! Yeah! Yeah! Yeah!
Singin' Pharaoh, Pharaoh Oh baby! Let my people go!
Yeah! Yeah! Yeah! Yeah!

5. Telling The Story of Passover

Now a "Major" Motion Picture →

MAGGID:
The Story Of Passover

By
Rabbi Ben Screenwriter

Aug 12, 5782
Ver 712

CAST OF CHARACTERS*
(In order of number of lines)

PHARAOH (15 LINES)

NARRATOR 2 (13 LINES)

AARON (12 LINES)

NARRATOR 1 (10 LINES)

MOSES (8 LINES)

GOD (7 LINES)

PRINCESS (4 LINES)

PRINCESS' ATTENDANT (4 LINES)

MIRIAM (4 LINES)

PHARAOH'S SON (2 LINES)

SLAVE (2 LINES)

SHEEP (2 LINES)

HERALD (1 LINE)

YOCHEVED (1 LINE)

*Casting should be done completely blind of all gender, age, and/or classic "beauty" bias, to avoid any level of prejudice. Raw talent, on the other hand, should be considered.

EXT. DESERT - DAY

OPEN ON a hot, sandy desert. The sun beats down on shvitzing Jews, dressed in shmatas.

NARRATOR 1
The story of Moses and the Exodus from Egypt has been told thousands of times. It's a reminder to the Jewish people that once we were slaves in Egypt, but now we are free. And so, this year, as in years before, generation upon generation, we tell the story of Passover. Now, I invite you to relax and listen to this tale. We begin in Pharaoh's palace.

PHARAOH
Yes, I'll have more grapes. This morning I took a tour of all of my new pyramids and I'm totally exhausted.

SLAVE
Yes, Your Highness. I must tell you that as a slave, we are really doing a fine job at building those pyramids. Carrying bricks is just the discipline that my fourteen sons need.

PHARAOH
Fourteen? Did you say fourteen sons?

SLAVE
Indeed I did, Your Most Fabulousness.

PHARAOH
Leave my quarters. I've gotta think. This could be bad, really bad. I mean, I love having these Hebrew slaves, but there are just so many of them! They are not Egyptians, and as shocking as it might be, I don't think they even like me. What if there's a war and they join my enemies and fight against me? I am going to try to find a way to decrease this Jewish-Hebrew slave population.

HERALD

Hear ye, hear ye! It is hereby decreed by Pharaoh, ruler of the land of Egypt, that any son born to a Jew is to be drowned in the Red Sea.

ALL

NOOOOOOO!!!!!

NARRATOR 2

Our story continues at the banks of the Nile River, where we meet Yocheved, a Jewish woman with a newborn son.

YOCHEVED
(Distraught)

Oh no! Did you hear about Pharaoh's awful decree? I knew he was mean, but now he's killing our babies?! I need to hide my beautiful baby boy.

NARRATOR 2

So Yocheved wove a basket of reeds (which is another word for long bamboo-like sticks), put her son into it and hid it in the tall grass by the river. She then sent her young daughter, Miriam, to hide nearby and keep watch. The Pharaoh's daughter, who was a princess, eventually came down to the water to bathe and heard cries coming from the river.

PRINCESS

What is this?

PRINCESS' ATTENDANT

It appears to be a baby, Your Highness.

PRINCESS

A baby?

PRINCESS' ATTENDANT

Why, yes, Your Highness.

NARRATOR 2
She pulled the baby out of the water.

PRINCESS
Oh, it must be one of those Jewish babies that my dad, the Pharaoh, wants to kill. But look at this little guy. He seems so beautiful and innocent. I know, I'll take him home and raise him as my son. He will love me and respect me as his mother.

PRINCESS' ATTENDANT
As you wish.

MIRIAM
(As she comes out of her hiding place)
Excuse me, your highness, but would you like me to call a Hebrew woman to nurse the baby, so that your attendant can continue to tend to you instead of being distracted by the baby?

PRINCESS
Good idea. I hadn't thought of that. All right, your Hebrew woman may nurse my child, and when he is old enough to walk, she shall bring him to the palace for me to raise. I am going to name him Moses, which means "drawn from the water."

PRINCESS' ATTENDANT
Whatever you say, Your Highness.

NARRATOR 1
And so Yocheved's son, Moses, grew up as the Pharaoh's adopted grandson, with all the riches and prestige that such a position entailed. But when he was young, Yocheved told Moses that he was Jewish, so he always had great compassion for the Hebrew slaves. One day, he came upon an Egyptian guard beating an old Jewish slave. Moses got so angry that he killed the guard. Of course, by doing so he was breaking the law. He feared the consequences, so he ran away from the palace into the desert, and became a shepherd. That's where we pick up the story now.

SHEEP

Baaaaaaaaaaaaaaaaaaaaaaaaaaaaaaaaa…

NARRATOR 2

One fine morning, one of Moses' sheep strayed a bit from the path.

SHEEP

I said, "Baaaa!"

NARRATOR 2

Moses followed the sheep and came across a burning bush. It was the craziest thing. This green bush was on fire, but instead of burning up and getting all crinkled and then black, it stayed green. This was, of course, a miracle. It was God getting Moses'
attention so that he could talk to him. It worked.

GOD

Moses! Moses!

MOSES

Here I am.

GOD

I am the God of thy father, the God of Abraham, the God of Isaac and the God of Jacob. I have seen the affliction of my people in Egypt and have heard their cry. I have come to deliver them out of the hands of the Egyptians, and to bring them out of that place unto a good land, flowing with milk and honey. Now, Moses, I need you to go back to Pharaoh and tell him to let the Jews go free and then you will need to lead the Jews out of Egypt.

NARRATOR 1

It's important to know that Moses stuttered whenever he spoke, so he was always nervous to speak in public.

MOSES

B-b-but why should... I mean, why, why should I be the one t-t-to lead m-m-my people?

GOD

Fear not — I will be with you.

MOSES

What should I tell the people?

GOD

Just tell the Children of Israel, also known as the Jews, also now known as the slaves, that they need to listen to you, because you speak for me. Tell them to leave their homes and everything they have always known and follow you to the wilderness.

MOSES

That is crazy. They'll never listen and besides, I am slow of speech and slow of tongue.

GOD

You're right, it will not be easy. I forgot to mention Pharaoh is not going to simply agree to let his slaves go free. He will take some convincing, and it will not be pretty.

MOSES

Please send someone else.

GOD

Your brother Aaron speaks well, right? He will have to help. I will only speak to you, but you can tell Aaron what I said, and he can be the one who speaks to Pharaoh and the people.

NARRATOR 2

And so Moses and Aaron went to the people of Israel and convinced them that God had spoken to Moses. Then they went to see Pharaoh at the palace.

AARON

Pharaoh, we are here to demand, in the name of our all-powerful and all-knowing God, that you release the Hebrew people from bondage.

PHARAOH

LOL. That is really amusing, guys. So, Moses, back after all of these years to bring shame on your own house and your own grandfather?

AARON

You cared for my brother for many years. At one time, he loved you as a grandfather. But he is the son of a Hebrew slave. If you love him, you will let his people go.

PHARAOH'S SON

Moses! I missed you! (Looks at Aaron.) Hey, who are you?

AARON

I am Aaron, Moses' brother.

PHARAOH'S SON

I thought I was his brother!

AARON

Pharaoh, if you do not release the Hebrews, Egypt will be smote with a greater plague than it has ever seen before.

PHARAOH

There is no way I am going to do that! I don't know this God you are talking about, and I will not let your people go. Now get out of my palace!

NARRATOR 1

To punish Pharaoh for his refusal to let the Jews go, God turned the water of the Nile into blood. It was horrible. Everyone needs fresh water to live, and instead of water, the entire river ran red with blood. Pharaoh was furious, and he called Moses and Aaron back to the palace.

PHARAOH

OK, this is horrible! The Nile River has turned to blood, and it's your fault! Everyone is freaking out. Maybe your God is powerful after all. If I let your people go, will he turn the river back to water?

AARON

Yes, of course. We don't want to harm your people, we just want to leave and be free.

PHARAOH

Fine, then go.

NARRATOR 2

So Aaron and Moses left the palace and told the Jewish people to start getting ready for their journey. But then...

PHARAOH

Get Moses and Aaron back here!

AARON

Yes, Pharaoh? We were just leaving.

PHARAOH

Not so fast. I realized that when you go I will have no one to build my pyramids. So, I have hardened my heart and changed my mind. You need to stay.

MOSES

B-b-b-ut Pharaoh, more terrible things will happen to the Egyptian people if you do not let us go!

PHARAOH

I will take my chances. Now get out of my palace, and tell the Jews to get back to work!

NARRATOR 2

Soon, Egypt was overrun with another of God's plagues... frogs. Wherever you looked, there were frogs all over the land. As you can imagine, it was awful. So Pharaoh called Moses and Aaron back to the palace and told them he would now allow the Jews to leave Egypt. But when they were ready to leave, Pharaoh changed his mind AGAIN.

NARRATOR 1

The next plague God sent was lice... people and animals all got lice. Then flies everywhere. Then cattle disease... so all the cows got sick and died, then boils... terrible blisters on everyone... then hail fell from the sky... big pieces of hail, as big as ping-pong balls. Then locusts, which ate the plants and all of the crops.

NARRATOR 2

So between the cattle disease, which ruined the meat, and the hail and locusts, which wrecked the crops, Egypt was in bad shape. People were hungry. Then came the plague of darkness. The sun never rose, and people were frightened and cold. The plagues were spreading fear and sickness across Egypt.

NARRATOR 1

But the crazy thing was, after each plague, Pharaoh would call Moses and Aaron to the palace and tell them that if their God made the plague stop, the Jews could leave Egypt. So God would end the plague, and then Pharaoh would harden his heart and change his mind, keeping the Jews in bondage. It was a mess!

PHARAOH

Who is this God of yours? How is it that each of these plagues only affects the Egyptians and not the Hebrews!? Get out!

AARON

Pharaoh, our God is all-powerful! We don't know what we can do to make you see that you must give in. We're warning you now that God has told Moses what the next plague will be. He's going to kill the firstborn of every Egyptian household, including your eldest son. Pharaoh, don't let this happen! Let my people go!

PHARAOH

I do not know your God, and I will not let your people go. Get out of my house! GET OUT!

NARRATOR 2

God then came to Moses and instructed him to have all the Jewish people slay a lamb and smear some of its blood on the doorposts of their houses. Then, when the Angel of Death flew over Egypt, he took the lives of all of the firstborn, except for those in the homes marked with blood. Pharaoh's own son died. It was devastating. The people of Egypt were mourning. Moses and Aaron went to Pharaoh yet again.

AARON

Pharaoh, the grandfather my brother once loved, we are truly sorry for your loss.

PHARAOH

Go away! Go away and leave me to my grief!

AARON

But Pharaoh, now that you have seen how powerful God is, will you let my people go?

PHARAOH

Be gone already! You and your people! You have ruined my empire.

NARRATOR 1

So Aaron and Moses left Pharaoh and went to the Jews.

AARON

Listen to me everyone! Remember this day... when you were able to leave Egypt, we were slaves and now we are going to be free and God will guide us out of here to the Promised Land.

MOSES

We must go fast! We must make food, but... but... we must go before Pharaoh changes his mind again.

26

AARON

He won't change his mind. Not this time.

MIRIAM

Moses, if we leave right now, the bread won't have time to rise.

MOSES

F-f-f-forget the bread, let's go!

NARRATOR 2

Most of the Jews went with Moses and Aaron. But some felt the whole idea of leaving their homes and going to some unknown land was crazy, so they stayed in Egypt. But meanwhile…

PHARAOH

I have just let my slaves all go. This is not good for the people of Egypt. All that my forefathers have worked for will vanish if I lose the Hebrew slaves. Who will build the cities? The entire economy of Egypt will collapse. It will be the end of an empire. I WANT THEM BACK!

NARRATOR 1

So once again, Pharaoh had hardened his heart. He got his army together and went after the Jews. Because they were walking and had a lot of kids with them who were slow walkers, the Jews had only gotten a few miles away from Egypt and they were really close to the Red Sea.

MIRIAM

Look! The Egyptians are coming! They will kill us all! They will work us to death! Moses, do something!

AARON

Don't be afraid. God has handled things for us before, and I don't think he would have made all those plagues just to have us die at the edge of the Red Sea now.

NARRATOR 2

Then God spoke to Moses.

GOD

Moses! Lift thy rod and stretch out thy hand over the sea, and divide it; and the children of Israel shall go across the sea safely.

NARRATOR 1

It was amazing. When Moses raised his rod, the water of the sea parted, and the Children of Israel walked across on the ground at the bottom of the sea. They were totally fine. But when Pharaoh's armies followed to catch them, the waters closed in and Pharaoh's armies were drowned.

MIRIAM

That was a miracle! We made it across the Red Sea! I don't know what God has in store for us next, but at last we are free!

NARRATOR 2

And Miriam took a timbrel (which is another word for a tambourine) in her hand; and all of the women went out after her with their timbrels and danced and sang. This kicked off a trek of 40 years through the desert.

NARRATOR 1

It was also when God started sending manna (food from the sky that tasted like anything you wanted it to) and sustained the Jews until they reached the Holy Land of Israel. But all of that is for another story. In the meantime, Happy Passover!

THE END

The Ten Plagues

As we rejoice at our deliverance from slavery, we acknowledge that our freedom was hard-earned. We regret that our freedom came at the cost of the Egyptians' suffering, for we are all human beings. We pour out a drop of wine for each of the plagues as we recite them to signify having a little less sweetness in our celebration. Dip a finger or a spoon into your wine glass for a drop for each plague. Tradition says that you do not lick your finger after doing the ritual because that's kind of cheating! These are the ten plagues:

1 BLOOD
DAM

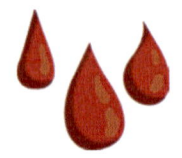

2 FROGS
TZFARDEIYA

3 LICE
KNIMIM

4 BEASTS
AROV

5 CATTLE DISEASE
DEVER

6 BOILS
SH'CHIN

7 HAIL
BARAD

8 LOCUSTS
ARBEH

9 DARKNESS
CHOSHECH

10 DEATH OF THE FIRSTBORN
MAKAT B'CHOROT

The Ten Plagues of Antisemitism

New Passover Tradition:

Seder Coffee - to wake us up to the Ten Plagues of Antisemitism

We have strong, black coffee on our Seder table

as a rallying cry for the Jewish community, and anyone who stands against hate, to wake up to antisemitism. We cannot ignore the danger faced by Jews around the world. Many of our ancestors came here as refugees, worked hard and contributed to society. And while there has always been hate, they were able to live good lives, and so have we. But the wave of antisemitism that is continuing to gain momentum threatens the ability of Jews to live safely and proudly. It is important to take the signs of hate seriously. Remember, it was the "paranoid" Jews in Europe in the 1930s who survived. Their foresight turned into action. We call upon that same willingness to take action now. It is once again time to wake up and fight like our lives depend on it, because they might. Reading the plagues is a good place to start.

(Take turns reading the plagues aloud while taking a sip of coffee.)

Plague #1: Silence
Remaining silent in the face of antisemitism normalizes hate. So does making it someone else's problem. No one has ever been antisemitic to me, so how bad could it be?" Well, very. Even if you haven't experienced it firsthand, your people have, your family has, your community has. Isn't that enough? All of our voices need to be loud and proud.

Plague #2: Non-Jewish Silence
Name the social cause and Jews are often standing out front supporting it. It would have been logical to assume that there would be many allies who would stand with the Jewish community during this time of great pain. Yet, this has not been the case. The treatment of Jews by our supposed allies is outrageous. While a basic Jewish value is to improve the world, it is important that Jews support the Jewish community, too. Standing up for others more than ourselves isn't the answer. We know that now. Please let's not forget.

Plague #3: Anti-Israel
Is Israel perfect? Of course not. But neither is any country. Still, again and again, Israel is the country that people are literally trying to erase from the map. There are forty-nine countries that have a Muslim majority and one hundred and twenty-six countries that have a Christian majority. There is only one country that has a Jewish majority. Why is there so much focus on this one country? Why is Israel held to standards that literally no other country in the world is asked to meet? It is because of antisemitism. The Jewish people need Israel. We've been kicked out of every country we've ever lived in, other than the United States (yet). The only place where Jews are truly safe from antisemitism is Israel. The Jewish people need Israel for our own safety.

Plague #4: Hamas
Hamas is a terrorist organization, not a resistance movement. Those who support Hamas are trying to dress up their Jew-hate as social justice. Hamas literally uses Palestinian civilians as human shields. Hamas also hates America, Christians, democracy, the LGBTQ community, women's rights and more. They might be starting with Israel, but they sure as heck aren't going to end there.

Plague #5: Hiding
We can't hide. It doesn't work. From tucking your Star of David necklace into your t-shirt, to letting an antisemitic slur slide, to not using your platform for good. If we assimilate out of fear and abandon our Jewishness, the bigots win.

Plague #6: Stereotypes/Scapegoating
Antisemitism has become so normalized that we may not always notice it. When someone says that Jews are cheap, or that our community doesn't need allies because we're all white/privileged, that's antisemitism. Conspiracy theories, like Jews controlling finance, the media, politics, even the weather, are used to blame Jews and encourage more hate.

Plague #7: Tolerating Hate
Jews are oppressors. Jews are all successful. American Jews are white and privileged. If the vitriol that is being leveled against the Jewish community was directed at any other marginalized group, people would not stand for it. But again and again, Jews are being singled out.

Plague #8: Schools
73% of Jewish college students have experienced antisemitic incidents since the beginning of the 2023-24 school year. How much more evidence do we need that campuses across the country are simply not safe for Jewish students? But the problem doesn't start in college. There are high schools, middle schools and even grade schools across the country where it is unsafe for Jewish students. There are antisemitic books being inserted into the curriculum of schools across the country. This is because those who are anti-Israel are working hard to move their agenda into places it does not belong. It's up to every Jewish adult sitting at this table to take action.

Plague #9: Social Media
Social media has become a cesspool of antisemitism. Wishing someone a Happy Passover on social media will be met with messages like: "Baby Killer," "Free Palestine," and "Hitler should have finished the job." There is no longer any space between antisemitism and Israel hate. If we are to have a hope of the next generation not hating Israel and the Jewish people, there needs to be an enormous correction of the way social media is handled and tolerated.

Plague #10: Small-mindedness
It is entirely possible to stand for the humanity of both Palestinians and Israelis. We do not need to be pro anything except pro-peace.

Dayeinu It Would Have Been Enough

One of the most beloved songs in the Passover Seder is Dayeinu. Dayeinu commemorates a long list of miraculous things God did, any one of which would have been pretty amazing just by itself. For example, "Had God only taken us out of Egypt but not punished the Egyptians – it would have been enough." "Dayeinu," translated liberally means, "Thank you, God, for overdoing it." Dayeinu is a reminder to never forget all the miracles in our lives. When we stand and wait impatiently for the next one to appear, we are missing the point of life. Instead, we can actively seek a new reason to be grateful, a reason to say **"DAYEINU."**

So, let's bring Dayeinu into the present.

We are grateful and yet what miracles and accomplishments would be sufficient (dayeinu) in today's world for us to be truly satisfied?

DAYEINU
Classic Version

Ilu ho-tsi, ho-tsi-a-nu, ho-tsi-a-nu mi-Mitz-ra-yim, ho-tsi-a-nu mi-Mitz-ra-yim, da-ye-nu!

If he had brought us all out of Egypt, it would have been enough!

CHORUS: Dai, da-ye-nu, Dai, da-ye-nu, Dai, da-ye-nu, Da-ye-nu, da-ye-nu, da-ye-nu!

Ilu na-tan, na-tan la-nu, na-tan la-nu et-ha-Sha-bat, na-tan la-nu et-ha-Sha-bat, da-ye-nu!

If he had given us Shabbat it would have been enough!

CHORUS: Dai, da-ye-nu, Dai, da-ye-nu, Dai, da-ye-nu, Da-ye-nu, da-ye-nu, da-ye-nu!

Ilu na-tan, na-tan la-nu, na-tan la-nu et-ha-To-rah, na-tan la-nu et-ha-To-rah, da-ye-nu!

If he had given us the Torah it would have been enough!

CHORUS: Dai, da-ye-nu, Dai, da-ye-nu, Dai, da-ye-nu, Da-ye-nu, da-ye-nu, da-ye-nu! Dai, da-ye-nu, Dai, da-ye-nu, Dai, da-ye-nu, Da-ye-nu, da-ye-nu!

DAYEINU
Contemporary Version

When all workers of the world receive just compensation and respect for their labors, enjoy safe, healthy and secure working conditions, and can take pride in their work... DAYEINU

When governments end the escalating production of devastating weapons, secure in the knowledge that they will not be necessary... DAYEINU

When technology is for the production and conservation of energy and our other natural resources are developed so that we can maintain responsible and comfortable lifestyles and still assure a safe environment for our children... DAYEINU

When the air, water, fellow creatures and beautiful world are protected for the benefit and enjoyment of all... DAYEINU

When citizens demand politicians who work honestly for the good of all... DAYEINU

When all women and men are allowed to make their own decisions on matters regarding their own bodies and their personal relationships without discrimination or legal consequences... DAYEINU

When people of all ages, genders, races, religions, cultures and nations respect and appreciate one another... DAYEINU

When all children grow up in freedom, without hunger, and with the love and support they need to realize their full potential... DAYEINU

When all people have access to the information and care they need for their physical, mental and spiritual well-being... DAYEINU

When food and shelter are accepted as human rights, not as commodities, and are available to all... DAYEINU

When no elderly person in our society has to fear hunger, cold or loneliness... DAYEINU

When the people of the Middle East and all people living in strife are able to create paths to just and lasting peace... DAYEINU

When the Jewish people no longer have to worry about antisemitism... DAYEINU

When people everywhere have the opportunities we have to celebrate our culture and use it as a basis for change in the world... DAYEINU

TOGETHER: If tonight each person could say this year I worked as hard as I could toward my goals for improving this world, so that one day all people can experience the joy and freedom I feel sitting with my family and friends at the Seder table... DAYEINU, DAYEINU!!!!!!!

The Second Glass of Wine

We recall our story of deliverance to freedom by blessing the second glass of wine:

בָּרוּךְ אַתָּה ה׳, אֱלֹהֵינוּ מֶלֶךְ הָעוֹלָם בּוֹרֵא פְּרִי הַגָּפֶן.

Baruch atah Adonai, Eloheinu Melech ha-olam, borei p'ree hagafen.

We praise God, Spirit of Everything, who creates the fruit of the vine.

6. Rachtza Hand-Washing (second): Preparing for the Meal

It's time to wash our hands again, but this time with the blessing. (It's customary not to speak at all between washing your hands and saying the blessings over the matzah.)

בָּרוּךְ אַתָּה ה׳, אֱלֹהֵינוּ מֶלֶךְ הָעוֹלָם, אֲשֶׁר קִדְּשָׁנוּ בְּמִצְוֹתָיו וְצִוָּנוּ עַל נְטִילַת יָדַיִם.

Baruch atah Adonai, Eloheinu Melech ha-olam, asher kid'shanu b'mitzvotav v'tzivanu al n'tilat yadayim.

We praise God, Spirit of everything, who commands us to wash our hands.

Another song!!!

🎵 JUST A TAD OF CHAROSET
To the Tune of "Spoonful of Sugar"

Oh, back in Egypt long ago,
the Jews were slaves under Pharaoh
They sweated and toiled and labored through the day
So when we gather Pesach night, we do what we think right
Maror, we chew, to feel what they went through.

Just a tad of charoset helps the bitter herbs go down,
the bitter herbs go down; the bitter herbs go down
Just a tad of charoset helps the bitter herbs go down,
in the most disguising way.

So after years of slavery, they saw no chance of being free.
Their suffering was the only life they knew
But baby Moses grew up tall and said he'd save them all
He did, and yet, we swear we won't forget that...

Just a tad of charoset helps the bitter herbs go down,
the bitter herbs go down; the bitter herbs go down
Just a tad of charoset helps the bitter herbs go down,
in the most disguising way.

While the maror is being passed,
we all refill our water glass,
Preparing for the taste that turns us red
Although maror seems full of minuses,
it sure does clear our sinuses
But, what's to do? It's hard to be a Jew!

Just a tad of charoset helps the bitter herbs go down,
the bitter herbs go down; the bitter herbs go down
Just a tad of charoset helps the bitter herbs go down,
in the most disguising way.

7. Motzi Matzah - Eating the Matzah

Raise the matzah and recite two blessings: the regular bread blessing and then one specifically mentioning the mitzvah of eating matzah at Passover.

בָּרוּךְ אַתָּה ה', אֱלֹהֵינוּ מֶלֶךְ הָעוֹלָם הַמּוֹצִיא לֶחֶם מִן הָאָרֶץ.

Baruch atah Adonai, Eloheinu Melech ha-olam, hamotzi lechem min ha-aretz.

We praise God, Spirit of Everything, who brings bread from the land.

בָּרוּךְ אַתָּה ה', אֱלֹהֵינוּ מֶלֶךְ הָעוֹלָם, אֲשֶׁר קִדְּשָׁנוּ בְּמִצְוֹתָיו וְצִוָּנוּ עַל אֲכִילַת מַצָּה.

Baruch atah Adonai, Eloheinu Melech ha-olam, asher kid'shanu b'mitzvotav v'tzivanu al achilat matzah.

Blessed are You, Spirit of Everything, who commands us to eat matzah.

8. Maror - The Bitter Herbs

בָּרוּךְ אַתָּה ה', אֱלֹהֵינוּ מֶלֶךְ הָעוֹלָם, אֲשֶׁר קִדְּשָׁנוּ בְּמִצְוֹתָיו וְצִוָּנוּ עַל אֲכִילַת מָרוֹר.

Baruch atah Adonai, Eloheinu Melech ha-olam, asher kid'shanu b'mitzvotav v'tzivanu al achilat maror.

Blessed are You, Spirit of Everything, who commands us to eat bitter herbs.

9. Koreich - Matzah Sandwich

Also known as The Hillel Sandwich, Hillel, an important Jewish sage who lived over two thousand years ago, is thought to have originated this tradition, which is why it is also known as the Hillel sandwich. The original recipe was a slice of paschal lamb, and a bitter herb. Jews no longer sacrifice a lamb, so now the Passover sandwich is made of matzah, charoset, and a bitter herb. The mixture is said to represent the sweetness and hardships of life.

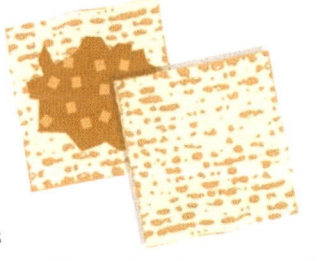

10. Shulchan Oreich - The Meal

DINNER CONVERSATION!
What's Your Superpower?

Instead of making small talk with the person next to you, try this with the whole table... We all have a superpower! It can be a natural talent (maybe you tell a great joke), or one that you've worked on (making a perfect cappuccino), or something more innate and subtle (you can keep a secret no matter what). What matters is that it's something you share with the world and which makes a difference to the people you share it with. What's yours?

11. Tzafun The Afikomen

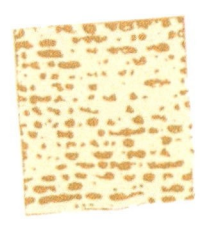

The half matzah, which was hidden earlier, now needs to be found.

NOTE TO CHILDREN:
The Seder CANNOT continue without it. This heavy task is on your shoulders!

12. Bareich Grace After the Meal

Baruch atah Adonai Eloheinu melech ha'olam, hazan et ha'olam kulo b'tuvo b'chen b'chesed w'rachamin. Hu noten lechem l'chol basar ki l'olam chasdo. Uv'tuvo hagadol tamid lo chasar lanu v'al yech'sar lanu mazon l'olam va'ed. Ba'avur sh'mo hagadol ki hu zan um'farnes lakol umetiv lakol umechin mazon l'chol b'riyotav asher bara. Baruch atah Adonai hazan et hakol.

We praise God, Spirit of Everything, whose goodness sustains the world. You are the origin of love and compassion, the source of bread for all, food for everyone. As it says in the Torah, "When you have eaten and are satisfied, we thank you for the earth and for its sustenance. Renew our spiritual center in our time. May the source of peace grant peace to us, to the Jewish people, and to the entire world. Amen."

The Third Glass of Wine

The blessing over the meal is immediately followed by another blessing over the wine.

בָּרוּךְ אַתָּה ה', אֱלֹהֵינוּ מֶלֶךְ הָעוֹלָם בּוֹרֵא פְּרִי הַגָּפֶן.

Baruch atah Adonai, Eloheinu Melech ha-olam, borei p'ree hagafen.

We praise God, Spirit of Everything, who creates the fruit of the vine.

13. Hallel Singing Songs

Echad Mi Yodea? Who Knows One?

Directions for Who Knows One:
Leader: assign the first who knows one, to someone. So something like: "Joe, who knows one?" And Joe says, "I know one. One is our God in heaven and on earth. Then, leader says, "Sue, who knows two?" Sue says, "I know two. Two are the tablets of the covenant." And Joe says, "One is our God in heaven and on earth." Then leader says, "Who knows three? Gary!" And Gary says, "I know three. Three are the patriarchs." And Sue says, "Two are the tablets of the covenant." And Joe says, "One is our God in heaven and on earth." And on and on and on… And you do it fast. And people always forget when it is their turn. And since we have already had HOW MANY cups of wine… Well, ya know… Anyway, have fun with it!

Who knows one? I know one!

One is our God in heaven and earth.

Two are the tablets of the covenant.

Three are the patriarchs.

Four are the matriarchs.

Five are the books of the Torah.

Six are the sections of the Mishnah.

Seven are the days of the week.

Eight are the days to circumcision.

Nine are the months to childbirth.

Ten are the commandments at Sinai.

Eleven are the stars in Joseph's dream.

Twelve are the tribes of Israel.

Thirteen are the attributes of God.

CHAD GADYA
Just One Goat

CHAD GADYA, CHAD GADYA dizabin aba bitrei zuzei, chad gadya, chad gadya. Va'ata shunra, ve'achla legadya dizabin aba bitrei zuzei, chad gadya, chad gadya.

An only kid! An only kid! My father bought for two zuzim. Chad gadya, chad gadya.

Then came the cat and ate the kid my father bought for two zuzim. Chad gadya, chad gadya.

Then came the dog and bit the cat. That ate the kid my father bought for two zuzim. Chad gadya, chad gadya.

Then came the stick and beat the dog. That bit the cat that ate the kid my father bought for two zuzim. Chad gadya, chad gadya.

Then came the fire and burned the stick. That beat the dog that bit the cat that ate the kid. My father bought for two zuzim. Chad gadya, chad gadya.

Then came the water and quenched the fire that burned the stick that beat the dog, that bit the cat that ate the kid. My father bought for two zuzim. Chad gadya, chad gadya.

Then came the ox and drank the water that quenched the fire that burned the stick, that beat the dog that bit the cat, that ate the kid my father bought for two zuzim. Chad gadya, chad gadya.

Then came the butcher and killed the ox. Then came the ox and drank the water. That quenched the fire that burned the stick. That beat the dog that bit the cat that ate the kid my father bought for two zuzim. Chad gadya, chad gadya.

Then came the angel of death and slew the butcher. Then came the butcher and killed the ox. Then came the ox and drank the water, that quenched the fire, that burned the stick, that beat the dog that bit the cat, that ate the kid my father bought for two zuzim Chad gadya, chad gadya.

Then came the Holy One, blessed be He! And destroyed the angel of death. Then came the angel of death and slew the butcher. Then came the butcher and killed the ox. Then came the ox and drank the water. That quenched the fire that burned the stick, that beat the dog that bit the cat, that ate the kid my father bought for two zuzim. Chad gadya, chad gadya.

The Fourth Glass of Wine

בָּרוּךְ אַתָּה ה׳, אֱלֹהֵינוּ מֶלֶךְ הָעוֹלָם בּוֹרֵא פְּרִי הַגָּפֶן.

Baruch atah Adonai, Eloheinu Melech ha-olam, borei p'ree hagafen.

We praise God, Spirit of Everything, who creates the fruit of the vine.

Elijah's Cup

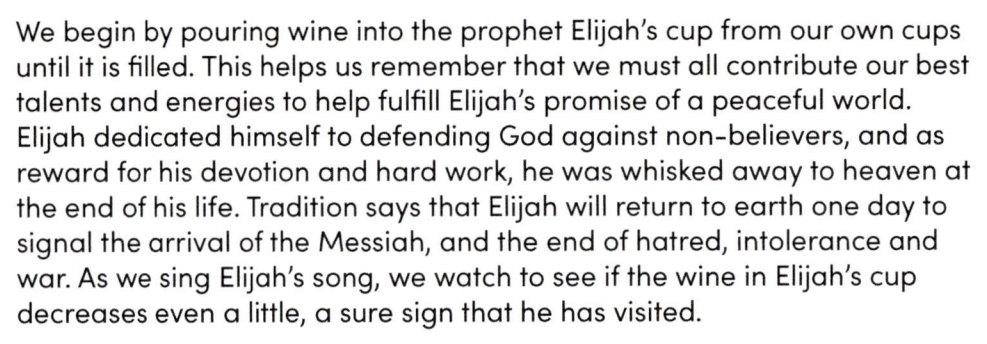

We begin by pouring wine into the prophet Elijah's cup from our own cups until it is filled. This helps us remember that we must all contribute our best talents and energies to help fulfill Elijah's promise of a peaceful world. Elijah dedicated himself to defending God against non-believers, and as reward for his devotion and hard work, he was whisked away to heaven at the end of his life. Tradition says that Elijah will return to earth one day to signal the arrival of the Messiah, and the end of hatred, intolerance and war. As we sing Elijah's song, we watch to see if the wine in Elijah's cup decreases even a little, a sure sign that he has visited.

אֵלִיָּהוּ הַנָּבִיא, אֵלִיָּהוּ הַתִּשְׁבִּי, אֵלִיָּהוּ, אֵלִיָּהוּ, אֵלִיָּהוּ הַגִּלְעָדִי. בִּמְהֵרָה בְיָמֵינוּ, יָבֹא אֵלֵינוּ, עִם מָשִׁיחַ בֶּן דָּוִד, עִם מָשִׁיחַ בֶּן דָּוִד.

Eliyahu hanavi Eliyahu hatishbi Eliyahu, Eliyahu, Eliyahu hagiladi
Bimheirah b'yameinu, Yavo eileinu Im mashiach ben-David
Im mashiach ben-David.

**Elijah the prophet, the returning, the man of Gilad:
return to us speedily, in our days with the messiah, son of David.**

Miriam's Cup

Miriam's cup is filled with water to symbolize Miriam's Well, a magical source of water that lasted during the 40 years the Jews spent wandering in the desert. We also honor Miriam's role in liberating the Jewish people, first by saving Moses from death on the Nile and then helping to raise him. Miriam's cup also celebrates the critical role of all Jewish women, past and present.

TOGETHER:
This is the Cup of Miriam, to symbolize the water which gave new life to Israel as we struggled with ourselves in the wilderness. Blessed are You, Spirit of the Universe, who sustains us with endless possibilities, and enables us to reach a new place.

🎵 I COULD HAVE EATEN MORE
To the Tune of "I Could Have Danced All Night"

I could have eaten more,
I could have eaten more,
But it's afikomen time.

The Seder rituals
And all those victuals,
The evening was sublime.
I had my matzah with charoset
And matzah dipped in chocolate too.

I drank down all my wine
And now I'm feeling fine.
How good to share this meal with you!

Credit: Irvine Sobelman, Jenny Sobelman & Martha Ackelsberg

THE SEDER CONCLUDES

14. Nirtzah
Ending the Seder and Thinking About the Future

We refill our wine glasses one last time.

בָּרוּךְ אַתָּה ה', אֱלֹהֵינוּ מֶלֶךְ הָעוֹלָם בּוֹרֵא פְּרִי הַגָּפֶן.

Baruch atah Adonai, Eloheinu Melech ha-olam, borei p'ree hagafen.

We praise God, Spirit of Everything, who creates the fruit of the vine.

L'shana haba-ah biy'rushalayim!
"Next year in Jerusalem!"

Made in the USA
Las Vegas, NV
02 April 2025